Anna AND HER Mommy

Gina Champion

Illustrations by Nanci Mitchell

Print information available on the last page

Rev. date: 10/08/2019

Published by Odenwald Press
Dallas / Panama City, Florida

ISBN 1-88463-20-2

To order additional copies of this book, contact:
Xlibris
1-888-795-4274
www.Xlibris.com
Orders@Xlibris.com

Note to Parents / Teachers:

The purpose of this book is to help children (age 4-8) differentiate themselves from their mentally ill parents.

Story Outline

1) Anna realizes that she can't "fix" her mother.
2) Anna accepts Jesus into her life.
3) Anna attains her own personal identity separate from her mother.

Hi! My name is Anna

My birthday is next week.
I will be seven years old.

I'm glad not to be six anymore.
While I was six a lot of bad things happened.

This year my Mommy was very sick
She cried a lot and seemed very sad.

I would feel sad, too
I felt like my Mommy's sadness was my fault.

I tried to help her. I'd tell Mommy,
"It will be okay."

I'd tell her that I loved her.
But she was still sad.

Lots of times she would sleep all day,
and I'd try to wake her up before Daddy came home,
so she could make him supper.

I don't want Daddy to be mad at her.
Mommy was so sad and tired.
I was too.

Last year I started the first grade.

I was shy and scared.

One day my Mommy came to get me from school.
I heard the teacher tell her to get me some help.
I don't know why.

I thought that maybe I was sick like Mommy.
Daddy says that my Mommy is mentally ill.

Mommy took me to a big building to see a nice lady.

The lady told me that I was pretty and smart.
She asked me how I felt.
I felt sad just like my Mommy.

I saw her a lot, and she always asked me how I felt.
I don't know why.

She told me that I am not my Mommy.
And that I don't have to be sad and tired like my Mommy was.

I don't know why the lady said that
I am not sick like my Mommy.
But I do feel better.

Sometimes, when I see her,
she tells me how to talk to my friend—Jesus.
She calls it prayer.

She smiles. She's happy.

Last week she asked me if I'd like to know Him.
I told her that I would.

So, I prayed Jesus, thank you for loving me and dying for me.
I am sorry for the bad things I have done. Please forgive me.
I want you Jesus to be my friend and Lord. Amen.

Now I laugh.

I pray.

I am not sick like my Mommy. But, when I do feel sad,
I talk to my new friend, Jesus.

I am not sad like my Mommy.

I'm starting to like school.

I kind of like myself, too!
I smile more.

To have Jesus as your Lord and friend, pray —

Jesus, thank you for loving me. I am sorry for any bad things I've done.
Please forgive me. I want you, Jesus, to be my friend and Lord. I believe
that you died for me and I receive you as Lord. Amen.

Printed in the United States
By Bookmasters